THE COMPOUNDING BLUEPRINT

START SMALL. STAY CONSISTENT. THINK BIG.

SAKET RAUSHAN

To my father, Late Shri. Rajni Ranjan Sinha, whose wisdom and resilience continue to inspire me every day.

To my mother Smt. Nilam Sinha, and my wife Mrs. Jinisha Verma whose unwavering support and love have been my foundation.

To Alex Hormozi, Ali Abdaal, Ankur Warikoo, Steven Bartlett, Warren Buffett, Morgan Housel, Jay Shetty, Simon Sinek, and Ramit Sethi—your work has profoundly shaped my understanding of growth, wealth, and the transformative power of compounding.

To Alex, Jamie, and Taylor—the characters who embody the principles of growth, resilience, and compounding in every aspect of life.

And to every reader who dreams of building a better future for themselves and their loved ones, may this book serve as a guide and inspiration.

Lastly, I owe a great deal of gratitude to four books that have been pivotal in my journey:

Rich Dad Poor Dad by Robert Kiyosaki,

The Psychology of Money by Morgan Housel,

The Intelligent Investor by Benjamin Graham,

Feel Good Productivity by Ali Abdaal.

These timeless works illuminate the path to financial literacy, self-improvement, and purposeful living.

Contents

Contents

Foreword

Every so often, a single idea comes along that changes the way you see the world. For me, that idea was the power of compounding. At first glance, it seems like a simple mathematical principle—a snowball rolling down a hill, gathering more snow as it goes. But dig deeper, and you'll discover that compounding is not just about numbers; it's about life itself.

This book is the result of years of reflection, learning, and real-world application of this profound concept. It's a journey that started with curiosity and grew into a mission: to show how compounding can transform every area of our lives—our finances, relationships, skills, and even our sense of purpose.

When I began writing The Compounding Blueprint, I wasn't just thinking about investment portfolios or savings accounts. I was thinking about the kind of growth that enriches lives—how small, consistent actions can lead to extraordinary outcomes over time. Whether it's dedicating a few minutes each day to a new skill, nurturing relationships with the people we care about, or taking incremental steps toward financial independence, compounding has the power to create exponential returns in every area of life.

I've drawn inspiration from some incredible minds—visionaries like Alex Hormozi, Morgan Housel, and Warren Buffett, whose work has shaped my understanding of wealth and growth. But this book isn't just about their wisdom; it's about translating those timeless principles into stories, strategies, and actionable advice that anyone can apply.

You'll meet Alex, Jamie, and Taylor, three fictional characters whose journeys mirror the challenges and triumphs we all face. Through their experiences, you'll see how compounding can play out in different walks of life, and you'll come away with tools to build your own version of success.

The Compounding Blueprint is not a magic formula, nor does it promise overnight results. What it offers is a roadmap—one rooted in patience, discipline, and the belief that greatness is built through small, intentional steps over time.

As you turn these pages, I invite you to embrace the mindset of a long-term thinker. Start small, stay consistent, and trust in the process. Because the The Compounding Blueprint isn't just a principle—it's a way of life, and it's waiting to transform yours.

Here's to the journey ahead.

Sincerely,

Saket Raushan

Preface

Introduction to the Hero's Journey.

Meet Alex, Jamie, and Taylor. These three personas will guide readers through the principles and applications of compounding in various aspects of life. Each persona represents a different background and set of challenges, making the journey relatable and inspirational for readers from all walks of life. Alex, Jamie, and Taylor's stories are filled with triumphs, setbacks, and valuable lessons that will resonate deeply with readers.

Acknowledgements

Writing The Compounding Blueprint has been a transformative journey, and it would not have been possible without the guidance, support, and inspiration of several remarkable individuals.

First, my deepest gratitude to my family—my mother, wife, and loved ones—for their unwavering support, belief in my vision, and constant encouragement. You've been my anchor and my inspiration throughout this journey.

To my late father, Mr. Rajni Ranjan Sinha, whose life and values continue to guide me—this book is a testament to the lessons you taught me about resilience, perseverance, and the importance of investing in what truly matters.

I am profoundly grateful to the thought leaders whose wisdom has shaped my understanding of compounding and personal growth: Alex Hormozi, Ali Abdaal, Ankur Warikoo, Steven Bartlett, Warren Buffett, Morgan Housel, Jay Shetty, Simon Sinek, and Ramit Sethi. Your ideas have been a source of endless inspiration and have enriched not just my knowledge but my life.

A special acknowledgment to the authors of the books that shaped my journey: Rich Dad Poor Dad, The Psychology of Money, The Intelligent Investor, and Feel Good Productivity. These works have been my guiding stars, offering clarity and insight at every turn.

To my friends, colleagues, and mentors, thank you for your encouragement, feedback, and belief in this project. Your insights and suggestions have helped bring this book to life.

Finally, to you, the reader—thank you for embarking on this journey with me. Your curiosity, dedication, and desire for growth are what fuel the principles in this book. My hope is that these pages inspire you to take bold steps toward creating a life of abundance and fulfillment.

This book is not just a reflection of my efforts but a celebration of everyone who has contributed to the power of compounding in my life.

    With heartfelt gratitude,

Saket Raushan

Prologue

Imagine a tiny snowball perched atop a hill. As it begins to roll, it gathers momentum, growing larger with each turn. By the time it reaches the bottom, it's transformed into a force of nature—far greater than it was at the start.

This is the essence of compounding, a principle that holds the key to exponential growth in every facet of life. But compounding isn't just about numbers on a spreadsheet or investment charts; it's a universal law that governs how small, consistent actions lead to extraordinary results over time.

When I first discovered the concept of compounding, I was captivated by its simplicity—and its infinite potential. It became clear that the same principle driving financial success could be applied to personal growth, relationships, health, and productivity. This realization sparked a journey of exploration, application, and eventually, this book.

The Compounding Blueprint is more than just a guide—it's an invitation to rethink how you approach success, one small step at a time. It's about unlocking the infinite potential of compounding in every area of your life and realizing that the greatest transformations often come from the smallest beginnings.

In the pages ahead, you'll meet Alex, Jamie, and Taylor—three individuals whose stories reflect the power of compounding in action. Through their triumphs, struggles, and lessons, you'll see how this principle can work for you, no matter where you're starting from.

As you embark on this journey, remember: greatness isn't achieved overnight. It's built on a foundation of patience, discipline, and a commitment to the process. The snowball is waiting to roll, and all it needs is your push.

Welcome to the The Compounding Blueprint. Let's begin.

CHAPTER I

The Compounding Blueprint

The Power of Compounding

Imagine a tiny snowball rolling down a hill. As it travels, it picks up more snow, growing larger and larger. This is compounding in action. At its core, compounding is the process where the value of an asset or effort increases exponentially over time. This principle is not limited to finances; it's a universal law that applies to every aspect of life.

The idea of compounding has been revered throughout history. Albert Einstein famously called compound interest the "eighth wonder of the world." Its power lies in its simplicity and the astounding results it can yield over time. Understanding this principle has been a cornerstone of wisdom for investors and thinkers alike.

"*Mathematically, compounding is expressed as $A=P(1+rn)ntA = P(1 + \frac{r}{n})^{nt}A=P(1+nr)nt$, where:*

A is the amount of money accumulated after n years, including interest.

P is the principal amount (the initial amount of money).

r is the annual interest rate (decimal).

n is the number of times that interest is compounded per year.

t is the time the money is invested for, in years."

While the formula may seem complex, the principle is straightforward: the longer you let your money, skills, or efforts compound, the greater the exponential growth.

Compounding isn't just for investors. It's a principle that applies to personal growth, relationships, health, and productivity. By understanding and applying compounding in all areas of life, you can achieve remarkable long-term benefits.

Alex started with a small investment in an index fund. Each year, Alex reinvested the earnings, allowing the investment to grow exponentially. Jamie, on the other hand, applied the concept of compounding to personal development by dedicating an hour every day to learning new skills. Taylor used compounding to build stronger relationships by consistently investing time and effort into their connections with family and friends.

\#

By embracing the principles of compounding, Alex, Jamie, and Taylor discovered the profound impact it could have on various aspects of their lives, setting the stage for a transformative journey.

• • •

CHAPTER II

The Role of Time in Compounding

Time as the Key Ingredient

Time is the critical component in compounding. The longer you invest, the more you benefit from exponential growth. Alex's early investments, despite being small, grew significantly over decades, illustrating the importance of starting early.

Starting early gives you a significant advantage. A small investment made at a young age can grow substantially more than a larger investment made later in life. The same applies to personal growth—small, consistent efforts over time yield monumental results.

Jamie began learning to code in their twenties. Although the initial progress was slow, the accumulated knowledge and experience over a decade led to a lucrative career in tech. Taylor, who started investing in their thirties, saw firsthand how even a ten-year delay compared to Alex resulted in a substantial difference in investment growth.

"Compounding requires patience. In the early stages, progress may seem slow and insignificant. But with time, the growth accelerates. Understanding this can help you stay motivated and committed."

Human psychology often struggles with the concept of delayed gratification. We're wired to seek immediate rewards. However, shifting your mindset to value long-term gains can help you harness the true power of compounding.

#

By starting early and being patient, Alex, Jamie, and Taylor maximized the potential of compounding, demonstrating the invaluable role time plays in achieving long-term success. Time, therefore, is not just an abstract concept; it is a tangible asset that we can use to our advantage. Whether it's the time we invest in our relationships, our health, or our finances, the sooner we start, the more we stand to gain.

• • •

CHAPTER III

Compounding in Personal Growth and Life

Continuous Improvement

Personal growth is a prime area where compounding can have a profound impact. Regularly investing time in learning new skills or improving existing ones can lead to exponential improvements over time. Each new skill builds upon the previous ones, creating a vast reservoir of knowledge and abilities.

Consider learning a new language. Initially, progress is slow and the effort feels immense compared to the reward. But as you continue, your vocabulary expands, your comprehension improves, and soon enough, you find yourself fluent. This compounding effect of skill acquisition can be applied to any area of personal development, from public speaking to coding.

Alex's journey in personal growth mirrors the principles of compounding. Small, consistent efforts in learning and self-improvement led to significant professional and personal development over time. Jamie's commitment to daily practice and continuous learning in their chosen field resulted in exponential career growth.

"Relationships also benefit from compounding. Consistently nurturing connections with family, friends, and colleagues leads to deeper, more meaningful relationships. These relationships, in turn, provide support, opportunities, and a richer life experience."

Health is another area where small, consistent efforts can compound into significant long-term benefits. Regular exercise, balanced nutrition, and mindfulness practices are examples of habits that can lead to a healthier, more fulfilling life. The key is consistency—small, daily actions that, over time, lead to profound improvements.

"Daily habits, no matter how small, contribute to long-term outcomes. Establishing positive routines can lead to significant life improvements. Imagine the impact of reading just 10 pages a day. It might seem inconsequential, but over a year, you would have read several books, vastly expanding your knowledge and perspective."

Taylor applied compounding to building relationships. By dedicating regular time to family, friends, and colleagues, Taylor nurtured a support network that provided emotional and professional support, enhancing their quality of life.

\#

Through consistent personal growth efforts, Alex, Jamie, and Taylor demonstrated how small, incremental improvements could lead to significant life transformations.

• • •

CHAPTER IV

Productivity and Compounding

Incremental Gains in Productivity

Productivity is another area where compounding plays a vital role. Small, consistent efforts in daily tasks can lead to substantial achievements over time. By focusing on incremental progress, you can build a foundation for significant long-term success.

One of the keys to productivity is breaking down large tasks into manageable pieces. By consistently working on these smaller tasks, you gradually make progress towards your larger goals. This is the essence of compounding in productivity—each small effort adds up, leading to significant results.

Alex found that enhancing productivity through small, consistent improvements had a compounding effect, leading to substantial achievements over time. By adopting productivity techniques like the Pomodoro Technique, Alex managed to accomplish more in less time.

Jamie discovered that setting daily goals and reflecting on progress helped in staying focused and productive. Taylor used time-blocking to allocate specific times for tasks, ensuring a balanced and productive workday.

"Small wins are essential for maintaining motivation. Celebrating minor accomplishments creates a positive feedback loop, encouraging continued effort and leading to larger successes. These small victories build confidence and momentum, making it easier to tackle bigger challenges."

Effective time management and prioritization are critical for leveraging compounding in productivity. Organizing tasks and focusing on high-impact activities can amplify the benefits of your efforts. Tools like to-do lists, calendars, and project management software can help you stay organized and focused.

#

Alex, Jamie, and Taylor's stories illustrate how small, consistent efforts in enhancing productivity can accumulate over time, leading to significant professional and personal accomplishments.

● ● ●

CHAPTER V

Financial Independence and Retiring Early (FIRE)

The FIRE Movement

The Financial Independence Retire Early (FIRE) movement has gained popularity as more people seek to achieve financial freedom and retire early. This chapter delves into the principles and strategies behind FIRE.

The FIRE philosophy is based on the idea of living frugally, saving aggressively, and investing wisely to accumulate enough wealth to retire much earlier than traditional retirement age. Compounding is at the heart of this philosophy. By consistently saving and investing, you can harness the power of compounding to grow your wealth exponentially.

Inspired by the FIRE movement, Alex adopted strategies to achieve financial independence and retire early. Through disciplined saving and investing, Alex demonstrated the power of compounding in achieving life goals.

"Effective saving and investing strategies are crucial for achieving FIRE. This section explores various approaches, including frugality, passive investing, and maximizing retirement accounts. Frugality involves being mindful of spending and finding ways to save money without sacrificing quality of life. Passive investing, such as investing in index funds, allows your money to grow with minimal effort and lower fees compared to active investing."

Maximizing retirement accounts, such as Public Provident Fund (PPF), Employees' Provident Fund (EPF), and National Pension System (NPS), can provide tax advantages that accelerate the growth of your savings. The key is to start early, be consistent, and take advantage of the compounding effect.

Jamie and Taylor also embraced the FIRE philosophy. Jamie focused on increasing income through side hustles and strategic investments, while Taylor prioritized frugal living and maximizing retirement contributions.

\#

The journey to FIRE is not without challenges. Understanding common obstacles and developing strategies to overcome them can help maintain progress and motivation. One of the main challenges is the temptation to spend money on short-term pleasures rather than saving for long-term goals. Developing a mindset focused on delayed gratification and long-term benefits is essential for overcoming this obstacle.

Another challenge is managing risk and uncertainty. Investing always involves some level of risk, but diversifying your investments and maintaining a long-term perspective can help mitigate these risks. It's also important to have an emergency fund to cover unexpected expenses and prevent you from dipping into your investments.

By staying committed to your goals and leveraging the power of compounding, Alex, Jamie, and Taylor achieved financial independence and enjoyed the freedom to retire early. The FIRE movement is not just about retiring early—it's about gaining the freedom to choose how you spend your time and live your life.

• • •

CHAPTER VI

The Power of Small Wins

Celebrating Progress

Small wins are essential for maintaining motivation. Celebrating minor accomplishments creates a positive feedback loop, encouraging continued effort and leading to larger successes. These small victories build confidence and momentum, making it easier to tackle bigger challenges.

Focusing on incremental improvements, no matter how small, can lead to substantial long-term gains. This section explores the psychology behind small wins and how they contribute to overall success. When you achieve a small win, your brain releases dopamine, a neurotransmitter associated with pleasure and reward. This not only makes you feel good but also reinforces the behavior, making you more likely to repeat it.

Alex learned to celebrate small victories, which boosted motivation and reinforced positive behaviors. This approach aligns with the compounding principle, where small, consistent efforts lead to significant achievements.

Jamie celebrated milestones in skill development and career growth, while Taylor acknowledged the progress made in personal relationships and financial goals. These celebrations created a positive feedback loop, encouraging continued efforts.

"One effective strategy is to break down larger goals into smaller, manageable tasks. By completing these tasks one at a time, you create a sense of progress and accomplishment."

Another strategy is to set specific, measurable goals. Instead of aiming to "exercise more," set a goal to "exercise for 30 minutes, three times a week." This makes it easier to track your progress and celebrate small wins along the way.

It's also important to celebrate your small wins. Take the time to acknowledge your achievements, no matter how small they may seem. This can be as simple as giving yourself a pat on the back or rewarding yourself with a small treat. Celebrating small wins reinforces positive behavior and helps maintain motivation.

\#

By focusing on small wins and incremental improvements, Alex, Jamie, and Taylor harnessed the power of compounding to achieve long-term success. Over time, these small victories add up, leading to significant progress and a greater sense of accomplishment.

• • •

CHAPTER VII

Saving Strategies for Wealth Accumulation

Effective Saving Techniques

Saving is the foundation of wealth accumulation. This chapter discusses the importance of saving and how it contributes to long-term financial goals.

One of the most effective saving techniques is budgeting. A budget helps you track your income and expenses, identify areas where you can cut costs, and allocate more money towards savings. There are various budgeting methods, such as the 50/30/20 rule, which allocates 50% of your income to needs, 30% to wants, and 20% to savings and debt repayment.

Alex's disciplined saving habits, such as budgeting and automating savings, played a crucial role in accumulating wealth. These small, consistent savings efforts compounded over time.

Jamie focused on reducing unnecessary expenses and prioritizing high-yield savings accounts, while Taylor leveraged employer-sponsored retirement plans and tax-advantaged accounts to maximize savings.

Another effective technique is automating your savings. By setting up automatic transfers from your checking account to your savings account, you ensure that a portion of your income is saved before you have a chance to spend it. This removes the temptation to spend and makes saving a habit.

"Reducing unnecessary expenses is also crucial for effective saving. This involves distinguishing between needs and wants and prioritizing spending on essential items. Cutting back on discretionary spending, such as dining out, entertainment, and shopping, can free up more money for

savings."

Building an emergency fund is a crucial aspect of financial planning. This section discusses the importance of having a financial safety net and strategies for building one. An emergency fund provides a cushion to cover unexpected expenses, such as medical bills, car repairs, or job loss, without dipping into your long-term savings or going into debt.

\#

A good rule of thumb is to save three to six months' worth of living expenses in an easily accessible account. Start by setting small, achievable goals, such as saving $1,000, and gradually build up your emergency fund over time.

By implementing these saving strategies, Alex, Jamie, and Taylor laid a strong foundation for wealth accumulation and took advantage of the compounding effect. Over time, their savings grew, providing financial security and helping them achieve their long-term financial goals.

• • •

CHAPTER VIII

Investing for Long-Term Growth

Smart Investment Choices

Understanding the basics of investing is essential for long-term growth. This chapter covers fundamental investment concepts, including stocks, bonds, and mutual funds.

Stocks represent ownership in a company and entitle you to a share of its profits. Over the long term, stocks have historically provided higher returns than other asset classes, making them a key component of a growth-oriented investment portfolio. However, they also come with higher volatility and risk.

By making informed investment decisions, Alex leveraged the power of compounding to grow wealth. Diversification and long-term thinking were key components of Alex's strategy.

Bonds are debt securities issued by governments or corporations. When you buy a bond, you are essentially lending money to the issuer in exchange for periodic interest payments and the return of the principal at maturity. Bonds are generally less volatile than stocks and can provide a steady income stream, making them a good option for conservative investors.

Mutual funds pool money from multiple investors to buy a diversified portfolio of stocks, bonds, or other securities. This diversification helps spread risk and can provide more stable returns. Index funds, a type of mutual fund, aim to replicate the performance of a specific market index, such as the S&P 500, and are popular for their low fees and passive investment strategy.

Jamie invested in a mix of stocks, bonds, and real estate, while Taylor focused on index funds and ETFs to minimize risk and maximize returns. Each persona tailored their investment strategies to align with their risk tolerance and financial goals.

"Compound interest is a powerful tool for growing investments over time. This section explores how reinvesting earnings can lead to exponential growth. By reinvesting dividends, interest, and capital gains, you allow your investments to generate additional returns, which can then be reinvested to generate even more returns."

Diversification is key to managing risk in an investment portfolio. This section discusses strategies for diversifying investments to minimize risk and maximize returns. Diversification involves spreading your investments across different asset classes, sectors, and geographic regions to reduce the impact of any single investment's poor performance on your overall portfolio.

Asset allocation is another important aspect of diversification. This involves dividing your investment portfolio among different asset classes, such as stocks, bonds, and cash, based on your risk tolerance, time horizon, and financial goals. A well-diversified portfolio can help manage risk and improve the chances of achieving your long-term financial objectives.

\#

By understanding and applying these fundamental investment principles, Alex, Jamie, and Taylor built diversified portfolios that leveraged the power of compounding for long-term growth. Over time, their investments generated significant returns, helping them achieve their financial goals and secure their financial futures.

• • •

CHAPTER IX

The Magic of Dividend Investing

Reinvesting Dividends

Dividends are payments made by companies to their shareholders, typically from profits. This chapter explores the concept of dividends and their role in investment portfolios.

Dividend growth investing focuses on companies that consistently increase their dividend payments. These companies often have strong financial health and a history of stable earnings growth. Investing in such companies can provide a reliable income stream and the potential for capital appreciation.

Alex discovered the power of dividend investing, where reinvesting dividends significantly enhanced compounding returns. This strategy provided a steady income stream and growth.

"One of the key benefits of dividend investing is the ability to reinvest dividends. Reinvesting dividends can significantly enhance the compounding effect. This section explores the advantages of reinvesting dividends and how it contributes to long-term wealth accumulation."

Jamie focused on building a portfolio of dividend-paying stocks, while Taylor reinvested dividends to purchase additional shares, accelerating portfolio growth. This approach provided both income and capital appreciation.

When you reinvest dividends, you use the payments to purchase additional shares of the same stock. Over time, these additional shares generate their own dividends, which can then be reinvested to buy even more shares. This creates a snowball effect, where your investment grows at an accelerating pace.

For example, consider an investment in a company that pays a 4% annual dividend yield. If you reinvest the dividends, your effective yield increases each year as you accumulate more shares. Over time, this can lead to substantial growth in both the number of shares you own and the total value of your investment.

Another benefit of dividend investing is the potential for passive income. Dividend payments can provide a steady source of income, which can be especially valuable during retirement. By building a portfolio of dividend-paying stocks, you can create a passive income stream that grows over time, helping to support your financial needs without having to sell your investments.

Dividend investing also tends to be less volatile than growth investing. Dividend-paying companies are often more established and financially stable, which can make their stock prices less susceptible to large swings. This can provide a measure of stability to your investment portfolio.

\#

By focusing on dividend growth investing and reinvesting dividends, Alex, Jamie, and Taylor harnessed the power of compounding to build long-term wealth and create a reliable income stream. This strategy helped them achieve their financial goals and provided financial security for the future.

• • •

CHAPTER X

Real Estate: Renting vs. Buying

Financial Implications

The decision to rent or buy a home is a significant financial choice. This chapter explores the factors to consider when deciding between renting and buying.

Financial implications are one of the primary considerations. Buying a home involves significant upfront costs, including a down payment, closing costs, and ongoing expenses such as property taxes, insurance, and maintenance. However, owning a home can build equity over time, which can be a valuable asset.

Renting, on the other hand, typically involves lower upfront costs and provides more flexibility. Renters can avoid the expenses and responsibilities associated with homeownership, such as maintenance and repairs. However, renters do not build equity and are subject to rent increases over time.

"Lifestyle factors also play a crucial role in the decision to rent or buy. For example, if you value flexibility and mobility, renting may be a better option. Renting allows you to move more easily for job opportunities or personal reasons without the complexities of selling a home."

On the other hand, if you plan to stay in one place for an extended period and want the stability of homeownership, buying may be a better fit. Owning a home provides the freedom to make improvements and personalize your living space.

Another factor to consider is the potential for appreciation. In some markets, home values have historically appreciated over time, providing homeowners with the potential for significant capital gains. However, real estate markets can be volatile, and there is no guarantee that property values will always increase. When evaluating the decision to rent or buy, it's important to consider your financial situation, lifestyle preferences, and long-term goals. Conducting a rent vs. buy analysis can help you compare the costs and benefits of each option and make an informed decision.

#

Ultimately, there is no one-size-fits-all answer to the rent vs. buy question. The best choice depends on your individual circumstances and priorities. By carefully considering the financial and lifestyle factors, Alex, Jamie, and Taylor made decisions that aligned with their long-term goals and helped them achieve financial security.

• • •

CHAPTER XI

Prepayment of Loans to Save Interest

Reducing Debt Burden

Prepaying loans can save significant amounts of interest over time. This chapter discusses the concept of loan prepayment and its benefits.

When you prepay a loan, you make extra payments towards the principal balance, reducing the total amount of interest you pay over the life of the loan. This can result in substantial savings, especially for long-term loans such as mortgages and student loans.

"Various strategies for prepaying loans are explored, including making extra payments, refinancing, and prioritizing high-interest debt."

Alex realized the benefits of prepaying loans to save on interest. By consistently making extra payments, Alex significantly reduced the overall debt burden.

One strategy is to make extra payments towards your loan principal. For example, if you have a mortgage with a monthly payment of $1,500, you could make an additional payment of $100 each month. This extra payment goes directly towards reducing the principal balance, which in turn reduces the amount of interest you pay over time.

Another strategy is refinancing. Refinancing involves taking out a new loan with a lower interest rate to pay off your existing loan.

This can lower your monthly payments and reduce the total interest paid. However, refinancing typically involves closing costs and fees, so it's important to weigh the benefits against the costs.

Jamie focused on refinancing student loans to secure a lower interest rate, while Taylor prioritized paying off high-interest credit card debt using the debt avalanche method.

#

Prepaying loans can impact long-term financial goals. This section discusses how to balance loan prepayment with other financial objectives.

While prepaying loans can save money on interest, it's important to consider your overall financial goals. For example, if you have high-interest debt, it may make sense to prioritize paying it off before focusing on lower-interest loans. However, if your loans have low-interest rates, you may be better off investing your extra money in a diversified investment portfolio that has the potential for higher returns.

"It's also important to have an emergency fund in place before aggressively prepaying loans. An emergency fund provides a financial safety net and ensures that you have access to cash in case of unexpected expenses."

By understanding the benefits of loan prepayment and implementing effective strategies, Alex, Jamie, and Taylor reduced the amount of interest they paid and achieved their financial goals more quickly. Balancing loan prepayment with other financial priorities helped them make the most of their money and build secure financial futures.

• • •

CHAPTER XII

The Impact of Frugality on Financial Independence

Living Frugally

Frugality involves being mindful of spending and finding ways to save money. This chapter explores the philosophy of frugality and its impact on financial independence.

Frugality is not about deprivation; it's about making intentional choices with your money. By prioritizing spending on what truly matters and cutting back on unnecessary expenses, you can free up more money to save and invest. This approach can accelerate your journey to financial independence and provide greater financial security.

Alex managed to save more money and invest in future goals by adopting a frugal lifestyle. This frugality played a crucial role in accelerating the path to financial independence.

\#

Practical Tips for Living a Frugal Lifestyle

Jamie and Taylor embraced frugality in different ways. Jamie focused on budgeting meticulously, ensuring that every dollar was accounted for, while Taylor explored cost-effective alternatives to everyday expenses.

"Budgeting is a fundamental aspect of frugality. A budget helps you track your income and expenses, identify areas where you can cut costs, and allocate more money towards savings. There are various budgeting methods, such as the

envelope system, zero-based budgeting, and the 50/30/20 rule."

Cutting unnecessary expenses is another key aspect of frugality. This involves distinguishing between needs and wants and prioritizing spending on essential items. For example, you can save money by cooking at home instead of dining out, buying generic brands instead of name brands, and reducing subscription services you don't use.

Finding cost-effective alternatives can also help you save money. For example, instead of paying for a gym membership, you can exercise at home or in a local park. Instead of buying new clothes, you can shop at thrift stores or participate in clothing swaps.

While frugality can lead to significant savings, it's important to balance it with maintaining a good quality of life. Living a frugal lifestyle doesn't mean you have to sacrifice enjoyment and comfort. It's about making intentional choices that align with your values and priorities. For example, if you value experiences over material possessions, you can focus on spending money on travel and activities rather than buying new gadgets and clothes.

It's also important to find joy in simple pleasures. By cultivating gratitude and contentment with what you have, you can reduce the desire for constant consumption and find fulfillment in everyday moments.

#

By embracing frugality and making intentional choices with their money, Alex, Jamie, and Taylor accelerated their journey to financial independence and enjoyed a more secure and fulfilling life. The impact of frugality extended beyond finances; it also led to a greater sense of contentment and well-being.

• • •

CHAPTER XIII

Leveraging Technology for Compounding Gains

Utilizing FinTech

FinTech offers various tools and platforms that can enhance compounding efforts. This chapter explores how technology can be leveraged for financial growth.

> *"Online banking and investment platforms make it easier than ever to save and invest money. Automated savings apps, such as Y1 Card, Zerodha - (Kite, Coin) and INDmoney, can help you save small amounts of money regularly without even thinking about it. Robo-advisors, such as Betterment and Wealthfront, use algorithms to create and manage a diversified investment portfolio based on your risk tolerance and financial goals."*

Productivity apps can help manage time and tasks more efficiently. Alex leveraged financial technology (FinTech) tools to automate savings and investments, enhancing the compounding effect. Productivity apps also played a role in maximizing daily efficiency.

Task management apps, such as Todoist and Trello, allow you to organize tasks, set deadlines, and track progress. Calendar apps, such as Google Calendar and Outlook, help you schedule and manage your time effectively. These tools can help you stay organized, prioritize tasks, and maximize your productivity.

"Online learning platforms provide opportunities for continuous education and skill development. Platforms like Coursera, Udemy, and Y1 Academy offer a wide range of courses on various subjects, allowing you to learn new skills and expand your knowledge at your own pace. Many of these courses are free or affordable, making education accessible to everyone."

Podcasts and audiobooks are another valuable resource for continuous learning. Apps like Audible and Spotify offer a vast library of audiobooks and podcasts on personal development, finance, productivity, and other topics. You can listen to them while commuting, exercising, or doing household chores, making it easy to incorporate learning into your daily routine.

#

By leveraging technology, Alex, Jamie, and Taylor enhanced their compounding efforts in various areas of life. FinTech tools helped them save and invest more efficiently, productivity apps improved their time management, and online learning platforms supported continuous education and skill development. Technology became a powerful ally in their pursuit of compounding gains.

• • •

CHAPTER XIV

Continuous Learning and Skill Development

Lifelong Learning

Lifelong learning is essential for personal and professional growth. This chapter discusses the importance of continuous education and skill development.

In today's fast-paced world, staying relevant requires a commitment to learning and adapting. Continuous learning helps you stay competitive in your career, opens up new opportunities, and keeps your mind sharp. It also enhances your ability to solve problems, make informed decisions, and innovate.

Alex committed to lifelong learning by consistently investing in education and skill development. This continuous growth had a compounding effect on personal and professional success. Jamie took advantage of online courses and workshops to stay updated in their field, while Taylor engaged in self-study and attended industry conferences.

Various strategies for continuous learning are explored, including online courses, workshops, and self-study. Online courses offer flexibility and convenience, allowing you to learn at your own pace from the comfort of your home. Many prestigious universities and institutions offer free or affordable online courses on platforms like Y1 Academy, Coursera, edX, and Khan Academy. These courses cover a wide range of subjects, from technical skills like coding and data analysis to soft skills like leadership and communication.

Workshops and seminars provide opportunities for hands-on learning and networking. Attending industry conferences, webinars, and local meetups can help you stay updated on the latest trends and best practices in your field. These events also provide opportunities to connect with like-minded professionals and expand your network.

Self-study is another effective strategy for continuous learning. Reading books, listening to podcasts, and watching educational videos can provide valuable insights and knowledge. The key is to be curious and proactive in seeking out information and learning resources.

"Establishing a regular learning routine can enhance the compounding effect of knowledge and skills. Set aside dedicated time for learning each day or week. This could be as little as 15 minutes a day or a couple of hours each weekend. The important thing is to make it a consistent habit. You can start your day by reading a chapter of a book, listen to a podcast during your commute, or take an online course in the evening."

Set specific learning goals to stay motivated and track your progress. For example, you might aim to complete a certain number of online courses each year, read a certain number of books, or achieve a certification in your field.

#

By making continuous learning a priority, Alex, Jamie, and Taylor enhanced their knowledge, skills, and personal development. The compounding effect of learning means that the more you know, the more you can build upon that knowledge, leading to exponential growth and improvement over time. Embracing the mindset of lifelong learners, they were better equipped to navigate the challenges and opportunities of the future.

• • •

CHAPTER XV

Building and Nurturing Strong Relationships

The Power of Networking

Strong relationships are crucial for personal and professional success. This chapter explores the role of relationships in achieving long-term goals.

"Relationships provide support, encouragement, and opportunities. Whether it's a mentor guiding you in your career, a friend offering a listening ear, or a colleague collaborating on a project, strong relationships can significantly impact your success and well-being."

Alex understood the importance of building and nurturing relationships. Strong connections provided support, opportunities, and a sense of community, all contributing to long-term success. Jamie focused on networking within their industry, attending conferences and joining professional organizations, while Taylor invested time in maintaining personal relationships with family and friends.

Various strategies for building and nurturing strong relationships are discussed, including effective communication, empathy, and networking. Effective communication is the foundation of strong relationships. This involves actively listening, expressing yourself clearly, and being open and honest. Practice active listening by giving your full attention to the speaker, asking questions, and showing empathy. Clear communication helps prevent misunderstandings and builds trust.

Empathy is another key aspect of strong relationships. Empathy involves understanding and sharing the feelings of others. By putting yourself in someone else's shoes, you can better understand their perspective and respond with compassion and support.

Networking is also important for building relationships, especially in a professional context. Attend industry events, join professional organizations, and connect with colleagues and peers on social media platforms like LinkedIn. Networking helps you build a strong professional network that can provide support, opportunities, and valuable insights.

"The compounding effect of consistently investing in relationships can lead to deeper connections and greater support networks. Investing time and effort in your relationships can create a positive feedback loop. As you build trust and rapport with others, they are more likely to support you, share opportunities, and collaborate with you. This, in turn, strengthens the relationship and creates more opportunities for mutual benefit."

Regularly check in with your friends, family, and colleagues. A simple message or phone call can go a long way in maintaining and strengthening your relationships. Show appreciation and gratitude for the support and kindness you receive. Small gestures, such as thanking someone for their help or acknowledging their achievements, can have a big impact.

#

By building and nurturing strong relationships, Alex, Jamie, and Taylor created a support network that enhanced their personal and professional lives. The compounding effect of these relationships led to greater opportunities, support, and fulfillment. Relationships are a two-way street—the more you invest in others, the more they are likely to invest in you. Being a good friend, colleague, and partner helped them build lasting connections that enriched their lives and contributed to their long-term success.

• • •

CHAPTER XVI

Health and Wellness: The Compounding Effect

Maintaining Good Health

Maintaining good health and wellness is essential for long-term success. This chapter discusses the importance of health and wellness in achieving life goals.

Good health provides the energy and vitality needed to pursue your goals and enjoy life. It also reduces the risk of chronic diseases and improves your overall quality of life. By investing in your health, you can enhance your productivity, mental clarity, and emotional well-being.

Small, consistent efforts in health and wellness can lead to significant long-term benefits. Alex focused on regular exercise and balanced nutrition, while Jamie incorporated mindfulness and stress management practices into their routine. Taylor made sure to get adequate sleep and maintain a healthy work-life balance.

Regular exercise is one of the most important habits for maintaining good health. Aim for at least 150 minutes of moderate-intensity aerobic activity or 75 minutes of vigorous-intensity activity each week, along with muscle-strengthening activities on two or more days a week. Exercise improves cardiovascular health, strengthens muscles and bones, boosts mood, and reduces the risk of chronic diseases.

Balanced nutrition is another key aspect of health and wellness. Eat a variety of nutrient-dense foods, including fruits, vegetables, whole grains, lean proteins, and healthy fats. Limit processed foods, added sugars, and excessive salt and alcohol. A balanced diet provides the essential nutrients your body needs to function optimally and maintain good health.

"Mindfulness and stress management are also important for overall well-being. Practice mindfulness techniques such as meditation, deep breathing, and yoga to reduce stress and improve mental clarity. Regularly taking time to relax and unwind can help prevent burnout and improve your overall quality of life."

The cumulative effect of healthy habits can lead to a better quality of life. Establishing and maintaining healthy routines is key. Start by setting specific, achievable health goals. For example, you might aim to exercise for 30 minutes each day, eat five servings of fruits and vegetables, or meditate for 10 minutes each morning. Break these goals down into smaller, manageable steps and track your progress.

Create a routine that incorporates healthy habits into your daily life. Schedule regular exercise sessions, plan and prepare nutritious meals, and set aside time for relaxation and self-care. Consistency is key to building and maintaining healthy habits.

\#

By making small, consistent efforts to improve their health and wellness, Alex, Jamie, and Taylor experienced the compounding benefits over time. Improved physical health led to increased energy and productivity, while better mental health enhanced their emotional well-being and relationships. Investing in health is one of the best investments you can make, leading to a longer, healthier, and more fulfilling life.

• • •

CHAPTER XVII

Time Management Techniques for Enhanced Productivity

Effective Time Management

Effective time management is crucial for productivity and achieving long-term goals. This chapter discusses the importance of time management and provides practical techniques for enhancing productivity.

Time management involves organizing and planning how to divide your time between different activities. Good time management allows you to work smarter, not harder, so you can accomplish more in less time and with less stress.

Various time management techniques are explored, including time-blocking, the Pomodoro Technique, and prioritization. Time-blocking involves scheduling specific blocks of time for different tasks or activities. For example, you might block out two hours in the morning for focused work, one hour in the afternoon for meetings, and 30 minutes in the evening for exercise. By dedicating specific time slots to different tasks, you can stay focused and avoid multitasking.

"The Pomodoro Technique involves working in short, focused bursts (usually 25 minutes) followed by short breaks (5 minutes). After four work sessions, take a longer break (15-30 minutes). This method can help maintain concentration, prevent burnout, and make tasks feel more manageable."

Prioritization is another key aspect of time management. Focus on the most important tasks first, rather than getting bogged down with less important activities. The Eisenhower Matrix is a useful tool for prioritizing tasks based on their urgency and importance. Divide your tasks into four categories: urgent and important, important but not urgent, urgent but not important, and neither urgent nor important. This can help you focus on what truly matters and avoid wasting time on less important tasks.

"Implementing a time management system can enhance productivity and compound personal growth. Start by setting clear goals and priorities. Identify what you want to achieve and the steps needed to get there. Break down larger goals into smaller, actionable tasks and prioritize them based on their importance and urgency."

Use a planner or digital calendar to schedule your tasks and activities. Plan your day, week, and month in advance, and allocate specific time slots for each task. Be realistic about how much time you need for each task and avoid overloading your schedule. Review and adjust your time management system regularly. Reflect on what is working and what is not, and make adjustments as needed. Be flexible and adaptable, as unexpected events and changes may require you to adjust your plans.

\#

By implementing effective time management techniques and creating a system that works for them, Alex, Jamie, and Taylor enhanced their productivity and achieved their goals more efficiently. The compounding effect of good time management led to greater success and fulfillment in both their personal and professional lives.

• • •

CHAPTER XVIII

Setting Clear and Achievable Goals

The Importance of Goal Setting

Setting clear and achievable goals is the first step in harnessing the power of compounding. This chapter provides guidance on goal-setting techniques and the importance of aligning goals with your long-term vision.

Goals provide direction and motivation. They help you focus your efforts, measure your progress, and stay committed to your objectives. Setting clear and achievable goals is essential for making the most of the compounding effect.

"The SMART (Specific, Measurable, Achievable, Relevant, Time-bound) framework for goal setting is explored in detail.

Specific: Your goals should be clear and specific. Instead of setting a vague goal like "get fit," set a specific goal like "exercise for 30 minutes, five days a week."

Measurable: Your goals should be measurable so you can track your progress. For example, if your goal is to save money, specify the amount you want to save, such as "save ₹4,00,000 in six months."

Achievable: Your goals should be realistic and achievable. Setting overly ambitious goals can lead to frustration and disappointment. Instead, set goals that challenge you but are within reach.

Relevant: Your goals should be relevant and aligned with your long-term vision and values. Consider why the goal is important to you and how it contributes to your overall objectives.

Time-bound: Your goals should have a specific timeframe. Setting a deadline creates a sense of urgency and helps you stay focused. For example, "complete a professional certification course within three months."

Aligning short-term goals with a long-term vision is crucial for compounding success. This section discusses how to create a cohesive plan that supports long-term objectives.

Start by defining your long-term vision and objectives. What do you want to achieve in the next 5, 10, or 20 years? Consider your career, finances, health, relationships, and personal development. Write down your long-term goals and break them down into smaller, short-term goals.

Create a roadmap that outlines the steps needed to achieve your long-term goals. Set milestones along the way to measure your progress and celebrate your achievements. Regularly review and adjust your goals and plans as needed to stay on track.

#

By setting clear and achievable goals and aligning them with their long-term vision, Alex, Jamie, and Taylor leveraged the power of compounding to achieve remarkable results. Goals provided direction, motivation, and a sense of purpose, helping them stay focused and committed to their objectives. The compounding effect of setting and achieving goals led to significant personal and professional growth. As they accomplished each goal, they built confidence and momentum, making it easier to achieve even greater success in the future.

• • •

CHAPTER XIX

Consistency and Discipline in Compounding

The Power of Consistency

Consistency is key to leveraging the power of compounding. This chapter discusses the importance of maintaining regular efforts in various areas of life and the role of discipline in achieving long-term goals.

Consistency involves making steady progress towards your goals, even when the results are not immediately visible. The cumulative effect of consistent efforts can lead to significant achievements over time. Whether it's saving money, exercising regularly, or learning a new skill, consistency is essential for compounding success.

Building discipline is essential for maintaining consistency. Discipline involves the ability to stay focused and committed to your goals, even when faced with challenges and distractions. It requires self-control, perseverance, and the ability to delay gratification.

One strategy for building discipline is to establish routines and habits. Routines help automate behaviors, making it easier to stay consistent. For example, if you want to exercise regularly, establish a routine of working out at the same time each day. Over time, this becomes a habit, making it easier to maintain consistency.

"Setting clear goals and priorities can also help build discipline. When you have a clear understanding of what you want to achieve and why it is important, it becomes easier to stay focused and committed. Write down your goals and

review them regularly to stay motivated."

Accountability is another effective strategy for building discipline. Share your goals with a friend, family member, or mentor who can provide support and hold you accountable. Regular check-ins and progress updates can help you stay on track and maintain discipline.

Challenges and setbacks are inevitable. This section provides strategies for overcoming obstacles and staying on track with compounding efforts. One strategy is to anticipate and plan for potential challenges. Identify the obstacles that could derail your progress and develop strategies to overcome them. For example, if you struggle with procrastination, set specific deadlines and break tasks into smaller, manageable steps.

Another strategy is to practice resilience. Resilience involves the ability to bounce back from setbacks and keep moving forward. When faced with challenges, focus on what you can control, learn from the experience, and stay committed to your goals.

\#

By maintaining consistency and discipline, Alex, Jamie, and Taylor harnessed the power of compounding to achieve long-term success. The cumulative effect of regular efforts led to significant progress and accomplishments over time. Consistency and discipline are not about perfection; it's about making steady progress and staying committed to your goals, even when faced with challenges and setbacks.

• • •

CHAPTER XX

Overcoming Psychological Barriers

Managing Psychological Barriers

Psychological barriers can hinder compounding efforts. This chapter explores the impact of psychology on achieving long-term goals and provides strategies for overcoming these barriers.

One of the most significant psychological barriers is the desire for instant gratification. Human psychology often struggles with the concept of delayed gratification, which can lead to impulsive decisions and short-term thinking. This section discusses techniques for overcoming the desire for immediate rewards.

Understanding the concept of delayed gratification is the first step. Recognize that many of the most meaningful rewards in life require time and effort. Remind yourself of the long-term benefits of your actions and stay focused on your goals.

Another technique is to break down long-term goals into smaller, achievable milestones. Celebrate these small wins along the way to stay motivated and reinforce positive behavior. For example, if your goal is to save ₹8,00,000, set milestones for every ₹80,000 saved and reward yourself with a small treat.

"Building a long-term mindset is crucial for compounding success. This section provides strategies for fostering a long-term perspective. One strategy is to visualize your long-term goals and the benefits they will bring. Create a vision board or write a detailed description of your future achievements. This can help keep your goals top of mind and motivate you to stay committed."

Practicing mindfulness and gratitude can also help build a long-term mindset. Mindfulness involves being present in the moment and appreciating what you have. Gratitude involves recognizing and appreciating the positive aspects of your life. These practices can reduce stress, increase happiness, and help you stay focused on your long-term goals.

Managing risk and uncertainty is another psychological barrier to compounding. This section discusses strategies for managing fear and uncertainty in pursuit of long-term goals. One strategy is to educate yourself about the risks and uncertainties involved in your goals. Knowledge can reduce fear and increase confidence. For example, if you're investing in the stock market, learn about the fundamentals of investing, diversification, and risk management.

Another strategy is to develop a plan for managing risk. This could involve diversifying your investments, having an emergency fund, or creating a contingency plan for potential setbacks. Knowing that you have a plan in place can reduce anxiety and help you stay focused on your goals.

#

By understanding and overcoming psychological barriers, Alex, Jamie, and Taylor harnessed the power of compounding to achieve long-term success. Building a long-term mindset, managing risk, and practicing delayed gratification helped them stay committed to their goals and enjoy the benefits of compounding in all areas of life.

• • •

CHAPTER XXI

Managing Risk and Uncertainty

Understanding and Managing Risk

Risk and uncertainty are inherent in many aspects of life. This chapter discusses the nature of risk and how to manage it effectively to achieve long-term goals.

Risk involves the possibility of loss or harm, while uncertainty refers to the lack of predictability or certainty about future outcomes. Both can create fear and anxiety, but with proper management, they can be mitigated.

Various risk management strategies are explored, including diversification, insurance, and contingency planning. Diversification is a key strategy for managing risk, especially in investing. By spreading your investments across different asset classes, sectors, and geographic regions, you reduce the impact of any single investment's poor performance on your overall portfolio. This can help protect your wealth and increase the likelihood of achieving your financial goals.

"Insurance is another important risk management tool. Health insurance, life insurance, and property insurance can provide financial protection against unexpected events and losses. By having the right insurance coverage, you can mitigate the financial impact of risks and uncertainties."

Contingency planning involves preparing for potential setbacks and challenges. This could include creating an emergency fund, developing a backup plan for your career, or having a strategy for managing personal or financial crises. Contingency planning helps you stay resilient and adaptable in the face of uncertainty.

Balancing risk and reward is crucial for achieving long-term goals. This section discusses how to make informed decisions that maximize growth while minimizing risk. One strategy is to assess your risk tolerance. Risk tolerance refers to your ability and willingness to take on risk. It varies from person to person based on factors such as financial situation, investment goals, and personality. Understanding your risk tolerance can help you make decisions that align with your comfort level and long-term objectives.

Another strategy is to focus on long-term growth rather than short-term gains. Investing in assets with the potential for long-term appreciation, such as stocks and real estate, can provide higher returns over time. However, it's important to balance these investments with more conservative assets, such as bonds and cash, to manage risk and provide stability.

Regularly reviewing and adjusting your risk management strategies is also important. As your financial situation, goals, and risk tolerance change over time, so should your approach to risk management. Periodically reassess your portfolio, insurance coverage, and contingency plans to ensure they align with your current needs and objectives.

\#

By effectively managing risk and uncertainty, Alex, Jamie, and Taylor protected their wealth and increased the likelihood of achieving their long-term goals. Understanding the nature of risk, diversifying investments, having proper insurance, and planning for contingencies helped them navigate the uncertainties of life and enjoy the benefits of compounding in all areas of life.

• • •

CHAPTER XXII

Learning from Failures

The Role of Failure

Failure can provide valuable lessons for future success. This chapter examines the role of failure in the compounding process and provides strategies for learning from failures.

Failure is an inevitable part of life. Everyone experiences setbacks and challenges, but how you respond to failure can make a significant difference in your long-term success. Viewing failure as an opportunity for growth and learning can help you build resilience and improve your chances of achieving your goals.

Analyzing failures can help identify areas for improvement. This section provides strategies for effectively analyzing and learning from failures. When you experience a failure, take the time to reflect on what went wrong and why. Identify the factors that contributed to the failure and consider how you could have approached the situation differently. This process of self-reflection can provide valuable insights and help you avoid making the same mistakes in the future.

"Seeking feedback from others can also be helpful. Ask for input from trusted friends, colleagues, or mentors who can provide an outside perspective on your failure. Their feedback can offer new insights and help you identify blind spots."

Turning failures into opportunities for growth is crucial for long-term success. One strategy is to adopt a growth mindset. A growth mindset involves viewing challenges and failures as opportunities for learning and improvement. Instead of seeing failure as a reflection of your abilities, view it as a chance to develop new skills and strategies.

Another strategy is to set specific, actionable goals for improvement. Based on your analysis of the failure, identify concrete steps you can take to address the issues and improve your performance. For example, if you failed a job interview, set a goal to practice your interview skills and seek feedback from others.

Resilience is also important for turning failures into opportunities. Resilience involves the ability to bounce back from setbacks and keep moving forward. When faced with failure, focus on what you can control, learn from the experience, and stay committed to your goals.

#

By learning from failures and using them as opportunities for growth, Alex, Jamie, and Taylor harnessed the power of compounding to achieve long-term success. Failure is not the end; it's a stepping stone to greater achievements. Embracing failure, learning from it, and using it to propel themselves forward helped them improve and achieve their goals more effectively.

• • •

CHAPTER XXIII

Case Studies: Success Stories of Compounding

Real-Life Success Stories

This chapter presents real-life success stories of individuals and organizations that have effectively harnessed the power of compounding to achieve remarkable results.

Warren Buffett

One notable example is Warren Buffett, one of the most successful investors of all time. Buffett started investing at a young age and has consistently applied the principles of compounding throughout his career. By investing in high-quality companies and reinvesting the profits, Buffett has grown his wealth exponentially. His investment philosophy, focused on long-term growth and value, has made him a billionaire and a respected figure in the financial world.

John D. Rockefeller

Another example is the story of John D. Rockefeller, the founder of Standard Oil and one of the wealthiest individuals in history. Rockefeller's success was built on the principles of compounding and strategic reinvestment. He started with a small oil refinery and reinvested the profits to expand his business. Over time, Standard Oil grew into a massive enterprise, and Rockefeller's wealth compounded to extraordinary levels.

"Analyzing success stories can provide valuable insights. This section discusses the key takeaways from various success stories. One key takeaway is the importance of starting early. Both Buffett and Rockefeller began their journeys at a young age, allowing them to leverage the power of compounding over a long period. Starting early gives you a significant advantage and maximizes the potential for exponential growth."

Another takeaway is the value of reinvestment. Reinvesting profits, whether in business, investments, or personal growth, can accelerate the compounding process. By continuously reinvesting, you create a snowball effect, where your returns generate even more returns.

\#

Patience and long-term thinking are also crucial. Both Buffett and Rockefeller maintained a long-term perspective, focusing on sustainable growth rather than short-term gains. This mindset allowed them to weather market fluctuations and capitalize on long-term opportunities.

• • •

CHAPTER XXIV

Practical Applications in Daily Life

Implementing Compounding Principles

Applying compounding principles in daily life can lead to significant personal and financial growth. This chapter discusses practical strategies for implementing compounding principles and monitoring progress.

One practical application is setting and achieving small, incremental goals. Break down larger goals into smaller, manageable tasks and focus on consistent progress. For example, if you want to build an emergency fund, start by saving a small amount each week or month. Over time, these small contributions will add up and create a substantial financial cushion.

Another application is automating your savings and investments. Set up automatic transfers from your checking account to your savings or investment accounts. This ensures that a portion of your income is consistently saved and invested, leveraging the power of compounding without requiring constant effort.

Habit formation is also crucial for applying compounding principles. Establish positive habits that align with your long-term goals. For example, if you want to improve your health, create a habit of exercising regularly, eating balanced meals, and getting enough sleep. Consistent healthy habits will compound over time, leading to significant improvements in your overall well-being.

"Goal setting and time management are essential for compounding success. Use the SMART framework (Specific, Measurable, Achievable, Relevant, Time-bound) to set clear and actionable goals. Write down your goals and

break them into smaller, manageable steps. Create a timeline for achieving each step and regularly review your progress. "

Implement time management techniques, such as time-blocking and the Pomodoro Technique, to stay focused and productive. Schedule specific blocks of time for different tasks and activities, and avoid multitasking. Regularly review and adjust your schedule to stay on track and make the most of your time.

Monitoring progress is crucial for maintaining momentum and achieving long-term goals. Use a journal, planner, or digital tool to track your goals and progress. Regularly review your achievements and adjust your strategies as needed.

\#

By applying compounding principles in their daily lives, Alex, Jamie, and Taylor achieved significant personal and financial growth. Practical strategies such as setting incremental goals, automating savings, forming positive habits, and managing time effectively helped them leverage the power of compounding for long-term success.

• • •

Conclusion: The Infinite Potential Of Compounding

The Journey Ahead

As Alex, Jamie, and Taylor's stories illustrate, the power of compounding can transform every aspect of your life. From finances to personal growth, productivity to health, the principles of compounding offer a roadmap to achieving remarkable long-term benefits.

The journey to harnessing the power of compounding is not always easy. It requires patience, consistency, discipline, and a long-term perspective. But the rewards are worth the effort. By making small, consistent efforts over time, you can achieve exponential growth and create a better future for yourself.

The infinite potential of compounding lies in its simplicity and power. By understanding and applying the principles of compounding, you can unlock new opportunities, overcome challenges, and achieve your most ambitious goals.

#

Key Takeaways

"Start Early: The earlier you start, the more time you have for your efforts to compound.

Be Consistent: Regular, consistent efforts lead to significant long-term benefits.

Stay Patient: Compounding takes time. Stay committed to your goals and be patient.

Reinvest: Reinvest your earnings, whether financial, personal, or professional, to accelerate growth.

Adapt and Learn: Embrace failures as opportunities to learn and improve. Continuously seek knowledge and adapt your strategies.

Focus on Long-Term Goals: Keep your long-term vision in mind and align your short-term actions with it."

\#

Final Thoughts

The Compounding Blueprint is within your reach. By embracing its principles and making consistent, intentional efforts, you can transform your life. The journey of Alex, Jamie, and Taylor is a testament to the incredible potential of compounding. Let their stories inspire you to embark on your own journey and harness the infinite potential of compounding to achieve your dreams.

\#

Embrace the journey, stay committed, and watch as the power of compounding transforms your life, leading you to success, fulfillment, and a brighter future.

• • •

Bibliography

This book draws inspiration and insights from a variety of sources, both timeless classics and modern perspectives, to craft a comprehensive guide to the power of compounding. The following works have significantly influenced the ideas and concepts explored in this book:
Rich Dad Poor Dad by Robert Kiyosaki
The Psychology of Money by Morgan Housel
The Intelligent Investor by Benjamin Graham
Feel Good Productivity by Ali Abdaal
Atomic Habits by James Clear
The Compound Effect by Darren Hardy
These works have served as valuable resources in understanding personal finance, growth habits, and long-term success principles.

\#

This book was created with a combination of personal insights, extensive research, and thoughtful writing. AI tools like ChatGPT were used occasionally to assist with idea generation and refinement. All content has been carefully reviewed and edited to ensure it aligns with my vision and voice.

• • •

Plan 1: Define Your Vision

What does success look like for you?

Take a moment to think about where you want to be in the next 5, 10, or 20 years. Define your long-term vision for your life. This can include your financial goals, career aspirations, personal growth, relationships, and health.

Prompt:

- What are your top three priorities in life?
- Describe your ideal future self in 20 words or less.
- What's one habit you can start today to move closer to this vision?

Plan 2: Break Down Your Goals

The Power of Small Steps

Big goals can feel overwhelming, but when you break them into smaller milestones, they become achievable. Use this page to break down one of your key goals into actionable steps.

Goal Planner Template:

1. Goal: (e.g., Save ₹10,00,000 for retirement)
   2. Why is this important?
   3. Milestones:

- ₹2,00,000 by [date]
- ₹5,00,000 by [date]
- ₹10,00,000 by [date]

   4. Daily/Weekly Actions:

- Automate monthly savings of ₹5,000.
- Track progress every quarter.

Plan 3: Track Your Habits And Progress

Consistency is Key

To harness the power of compounding, focus on consistency. Use this page to track one habit that aligns with your goals.

Habit Tracker Template:

- Habit Name: (e.g., Exercise 30 minutes daily)
- Start Date:
- Target: (e.g., 21 days of consistency)

Date	Completed? (✓/✗)	Notes
Day 1		
Day 2		
Day 3		

Habit Tracker

Reflection Questions:

1. What did you learn from tracking this habit?
2. How does it bring you closer to your long-term goals?

Plan 4: Compounding Reflection Worksheet

Seeing the Results of Your Efforts

Use this page to reflect on how compounding has worked in your life over the past months or years.

Reflection Prompts:

1. What small actions have you taken consistently? (e.g., Reading for 10 minutes daily, saving ₹500 a week)
2. What changes or results have you noticed? (e.g., Improved knowledge, savings of ₹25,000)
3. What motivates you to keep going?
4. What is the next area of your life where you can apply the power of compounding?